The Circle Model of
SHARED LEADERSHIP

By Elizabeth Fisher

Sponsored by Unitarian Universalist Women and Religion &
Unitarian Universalist Women's Federation

Published by Matrika Press

Copyright © Elizabeth Fisher and UUWR
The Circle Model of Shared Leadership

May 2019

All Rights Reserved
including the right of reproduction,
copying, or storage in any form
or means, including electronic,
In Whole or Part,
without prior written
permission of the author

ISBN: 978-1-946088-09-3

1. Feminist Theology 2. Women's Spirituality 3. Title

Matrika Press
164 Lancey Street
Pittsfield, Maine
04967

Editor@MatrikaPress.com

Matrika Press

www.MatrikaPress.com

Unitarian Universalist Women and Religion
www.UUWR.org

DEDICATION

Dedicated to Matilda Joslyn Gage
Born: March 24, 1826 in Cicero, New York
Died: March 18, 1898, Chicago, Illinois
Buried: Fayetteville Cemetery, upstate New York

Motto: *"There is a word sweeter than Mother, Home or Heaven. That word is Liberty."*

This important foremother was a founder of the Women's Suffrage Movement and author of *Woman, Church and State: A Historical Account of the Status of Woman through the Christian Ages with Reminiscences of the Matriarchate* (1893); adopted into the Wolf Clan of the Mohawk Nation; arrested for attempting to register to vote; an inspiration to L. Frank Baum, her son-in-law, when he wrote the Wizard of Oz books.

Also special appreciation goes to Sally Roesch Wagner for her commitment to educating about MJG. See the Matilda Joslyn Gage Foundation website for a fun tour through Gage's virtual home filled with insight and vision.

ACKNOWLEDGEMENTS

Thanks to UUs Bob Fisher, Patti Lawrence, Geri Kennedy, Rosemary Matson and Meg Bowman for their perseverance in bringing this circle model forward in booklets, workshops and their own leadership practices.

Also, we wish to recognize participants in the Women's Movement of the 1960s, 70s and 80s who passed these techniques around the many networks that built the foundation for the current resurgence of interest in participatory democracy and intersectionality that includes all voices.

TABLE OF CONTENTS

Dedication 3
Acknowledgements 4
Foreword 7
Women and Religion Resolution 9
Introduction 10
Systems of Decision-Making 12
Features of a Positive Meeting 14
Roles that Make Things Flow 16
Consensus Building 18
Conflict Resolution 20
Accomplishments *(Completing Tasks)* 22
Nurturing Relationships *(The Soul of the Group)* 23
How to Be a Good Facilitator 24
Benefits of Co-Facilitation 25
Example of Planning an Event 26
A Few Books to Consider 29
UUA Searchable Leader Lab Archive 30
About the Author 32
About UUWR and the Co-Conveners 33
Additional Resources 36
About Matrika Press

FOREWORD

The time is *Now*, like never before, to reverse the perpetuation of patriarchy that exists in all its forms within our own institutions, including how we function when it comes to decision-making and building beloved community. *The Circle Model of Shared Leadership* presented here affirms the inherent worth and dignity of each of us while supporting and facilitating cooperation among us. By using this method we strengthen our ability to live out our Unitarian Universalist values.

To bring this about requires mutual respect for one another and belief in the value of collective action. Used over many years by numerous diverse grassroots efforts, this form of leadership provides tools that enable successful group process while enhancing personal bonding. Flexible and adaptable, it is appropriate for the areas of stewardship, governance, membership, religious education, spiritual fulfillment and social justice movements.

One example of this power. In the autumn of 2017, thousands of our Unitarian Universalist sisters sent #MeToo messages in response to the outcries for radical change in how women are treated in society. This movement calls for the elimination of the legacy of sexual assault, sexual harassment, and victim shaming which has grown out of dominant/submissive leadership styles.

From this outpouring, the call to create opportunities to offer each other on-going reciprocal support as well as coordination of relevant education and public demonstrations was loud and clear. In communities across the country many committees did form, using, often without realizing, the shared leadership approach. The tips this book offers can aid these efforts and help new groups to form.

Unitarian Universalist Women and Religion (UUWR) participants are the creators of this book. We invite you to delve into this simple but powerful method by reading this book and adapting its suggestions to your own situations. Let others know about them also. Adopting these techniques can assist all of us in unforeseeable ways. Incorporating them into congregational functioning can make our collective life more cooperative and decisions more empowering for all.

WOMEN AND RELIGION RESOLUTION

UUWR dates back to the passage of the *Women and Religion Resolution* in 1977 by the UUA General Assembly, when Unitarian Universalists unanimously passed the Women and Religion Business Resolution. It emphasizes the responsibility to be prophetic messengers about the need to understand the relationship between religious and cultural attitudes toward women.

Over this long history there have been many local, district and regional W&R committees. One of the important characteristics of these has been sharing leadership and co-facilitating when planning activities and establishing support groups. Shared Leadership is one of the key ways over the years that the W&R Resolution has been implemented.

This Resolution calls on all of us to carefully examine and challenge cultural assumptions which cause women to be overlooked and undervalued. These include religious myths, historical materials, teachings and sexist language which can create sex role stereotypes that are often perpetuated in our own families, and even in our liberal congregations. These limit the sense of self-worth and dignity of each one of us.

The longstanding advocacies for the protection of women's rights as well as exploring feminist thealogy/theology are examples of the impact of this Resolution. For more than four decades we have been called to live into the UU Women and Religion Resolution and to do what we must to respond to needs when they become apparent. Fulfilling this Resolution continues to be an on-going process.

INTRODUCTION

This book is an easy-to-access presentation of the core ideas of *The Circle Model of Shared Leadership*, a dynamic facilitation process. By design, this discussion is brief in the hope you will start experimenting with these methods immediately rather than waiting until you have more time to "study" them. Many of these techniques can also be merged with traditional leadership models. Incorporate them into your already on-going groups to make them more participatory, effective and just plain lively!

The circle model suggests roles and techniques that encourage all members to become involved rather than relying on the charisma of a few leaders. By emphasizing communication geared toward mutual understanding, healthy groups thrive on lifting up the voices, knowledge and skills of all members. Rather than division and force, aka power plays, the group relies on nurturing relationships and consensus building.

When utilizing the well-structured participatory process presented here, both emotional connections and the efficient handling of tasks often results. This method holds harmonizing and compromising to be as important as initiating action. Aiding communication ranks with coordinating subcommittees.

Shared Leadership demonstrates a practical commitment to democracy and mutual respect. When this approach to community is adopted, those who have not felt comfortable participating because of the racial and cultural makeup of their congregations or organizations are given meaningful space in congregational life and institutional decision-making.

These tactics dismantle *Patriarchal Hierarchical Decision-Making* and empower the *Feminist Concept of Horizontal Process*. Rather than the *Power of Results* enforced by centralization of power, the focus becomes emphasis on the *Power of the Whole*. It helps us to listen to others, believing they may have unique perspectives that actually improve our own contributions. As members become comfortable with this variety, stronger bonds may form. Shared leadership also fosters more involvement by all those who attend a planning session, especially for an action, since each has taken part in shaping the event.

In this method, attending to the *soul of the group* is equal to goal oriented efforts. For example, you may want to try a "feelings check" at the beginning of the meeting when each participant can describe her or his current mood. And don't forget to use tension releasing activities like jokes, exercises or singing.

By taking the time to know one another's strengths and giving space for people to try something new, groups become capable of utilizing the variety of skills offered by each participant as well as strengthening the abilities of all. This does not mean participants do not acknowledge that their strengths differ. It does not mean jobs have to be continually rotated. It does, however, teach us the value of trying something different and allowing others to do so as well. This enhances the ability of the group to both achieve goals and provide one another mutual support.

These are just a few of the benefits the circle model has to offer. Explore and discover your own. The world is depending on our inventions and contributions!

SYSTEMS OF DECISION-MAKING

Old Hierarchy of Power
(aka Patriarchal Power)

Power of Results
Emphasizes programs, goals, or policies
that achieve the desired results.
Ends (achievements) justify the means.
"I don't care how you do it, just get the job done."

Power of Prescription
Imposes change by authority. Vested interests prescribe the
outcome. Paternalistic attitude:
"Do as I say, I know what is best for you."

Power of Division
Values centralization.
Knowledge and skills are hoarded by the privileged few:
"What they don't know won't hurt them."

Power of Force
Invests power for or against others.
"We're number one!"
Force is accomplished by a willingness to impose
penalties and negative sanctions.
One person makes decisions on behalf of the group.
"Do it or else!"

Shared Leadership
(aka Feminist Alternative)

Power of Process
Emphasizes fresh perspective
and freedom from rigid schedules.
Goals, programs and timetables are useful as tools,
but are less important than the process itself.

Power of Letting Go
Encourages change emerging out of
acknowledgement of a collective awareness.
Inspires balance between interests of individuals
and the group, self-knowledge and cooperation.

Power of the Whole
Values new ideas, images and energy from all.
Sharing of knowledge and skills is viewed as healthy and desirable
through mutual help networks.

Power of Collectivity
Values the personal power of each individual.
Consensus decisions are viewed as more viable
than those made by one person
or than those made by a voting majority.

FEATURES OF A POSITIVE MEETING

OPENING
Open with an appropriate short poem or song, or prepare a ceremony and light a candle or chalice, depending on the nature of the group and the topic of the gathering. This gets people "settled" and brings members together.

FEELINGS CHECK
Ask members, going around the circle, table or seating arrangement, to give their name and describe their current mood or something of interest going on in their life. This clears their mind so that they can freely focus on the group's agenda. This can vary from several sentences to just one word depending on the length and the tone of the agenda.

AGENDA
Prepare the Agenda in advance so that everyone has a copy. Or, write the Agenda on large sheets and post on a front wall. Or, write the Agenda in big letters on a Black/White Board. Or, have the Agenda projected on a screen or wall. Or, e-mail each participant a copy of the Agenda. Estimate times for each item. Start and close with the easier issues. Try to break large items into several, more manageable, issues.

BREAKS
Depending on the length of the meeting, schedule breaks. Also, schedule longer times, brunch or lunch perhaps, when members have a chance to informally visit. Use "light-and-lively" at least once or twice during your meeting.

EVALUATE
This can be informal, perhaps a feelings check about the meeting. This helps to provide closure and gives tips for how to improve future meetings.

CLOSING
To help make members feel connected and positive about the meeting, end with an upbeat or inspirational short reading, song or chant depending on the nature of the group.

INCORPORATING NEW MEMBERS
It is important to try to make new members feel at home. Give them information about the group that explains its purpose. Make sure more established members take time during the breaks to speak to new members and find out why they came, what their concerns are, and the focus of this particular meeting. When using acronyms or initials (such as W&R, UUWF, GA, UUA, BLUU, DRUUM, LREDA, UUSCM, UUMA, etc.) be sure the new persons know what they mean.

ROLES THAT MAKE THINGS FLOW

The following roles are designed to aid your group's functioning. Although most of these can be filled at the beginning of the meeting, it is preferable to have a facilitator(s) and recorder (scribe) selected prior to the meeting.

Facilitator (Convener): Compiles the agenda before the meeting. Moves the group through the agenda in the time available. Keeps the group on the topic. Points to agreements or possible compromises. Tests consensus or the need for further discussion. Co-facilitators are effective since they can help one another and keep a more watchful eye on the emotional tone of the group.

Recorder (Scribe): Keeps minutes of important decisions. If appropriate, can read back group agreements at the end of each agenda item.

Time Watcher: Keeps track of the pace of the meeting. If agenda items have been assigned specific time limits, the Time Watcher gives warnings with good humor when the time limit is approaching. The group then decides to finish discussion or extend the time.

Visual Aids Writer: If a Flip Chart or Black/White Board is used, the Visual Aids Writer prints "brainstorming" ideas, issues, future agenda items, summaries, decisions, etc. large enough for everyone to see.

Latecomer/Newcomer Watcher: Takes special efforts to welcome Newcomers. Collects any handouts and gives them to people arriving late. Greets any late arrivals at the door and quietly briefs them.

Who-Speaks-Next Watcher: Keeps track of who wants to speak; calling on each in turn. Participants who indicate that they want to speak can then follow the discussion without struggling for a chance to comment.

Light-and-Lively Leader: A "light-and-lively" is a quick tension reliever, mood lightener, song, body movement, or wake-up game. These should be humorous and energetic. When the meeting gets 'bogged down,' tiresome or conflicted, the Light-and-Lively leader shouts, "Light and Lively!" and asks everyone (as they are able) to stand and ... (choose from dozens of stress-relieving activities).

Process Observer: From time-to-time, a group can benefit from having someone observe how the shared leadership process is working. When reporting to the group, always point out helpful suggestions that were made or procedures that were used during the meeting that moved the group forward. Once the group has a sense of its strengths, it is easier to consider possible improvement.

MODELS OF LEADERSHIP

Contrasting Shared Leadership to other models is an easy way to see how this style works. Everyone has encountered the controlling style. Here a pyramid exists with a few occupying the top point. They make decisions that direct group activity without consulting everyone. Volunteer organizations will often reject this style. They will, however, frequently adopt the paternal style in which people at the top are nice rather than intimidating, pleasant instead of overpowering. Despite good intentions, the same governing philosophy dominates these organizations. Only a few people make decisions without adequate input from all involved. In an attempt to avoid these styles, many will form leaderless groups. These often fall apart, however, since many clusters may not need leaders but they do need leadership.
Understanding the differences between the role of the leader and the functions of leadership is the key.

CONSENSUS BUILDING

Consensus building does not use Robert's (or Roberta's) Rules of Order. Consensus is not competition between two groups (e.g., Democrats vs. Republicans) where the winner-takes-all, even if victorious by only one vote.

Consensus is a process for making group decisions without voting. Consensus is particularly useful to groups in which members highly value their personal associations.

To be effective, *consensus requires discussion(s)* based on a variety of information and viewpoints. Decisions reached by consensus are usually a synthesis of proposals or a new proposal developed as a result of the discussions.

Consensus does not mean unanimity. Individuals can disagree with a decision. Individuals can stand aside when they feel the implementation of the decisions will not violate their ethics or cause harm.

It's okay to take a vote. Decisions using the consensus process can still take a vote. Groups can then reconsider close votes, further processing the issue(s) using consensus techniques. Modified consensus procedures are often adopted by groups using shared leadership techniques.

In a growing, changing community *it is rare that complete consensus is achieved.* Remember that when an individual says "no" in the consensus process it is not a negative reflection on the community's mission, integrity, or caring spirit. It is simply an individual exercising the prerogative of free choice *(or just having a bad day)*.

Process is not the goal. Process is a means rather than an end. We hope that the consensus process will be a constructive use of community energy. The goal is to raise the level of satisfaction as opposed to lowering the level of dissatisfaction.

In your desire for *mutual empowerment,* use statements such as: "This is where I stand..." "What about this way of expressing ..." "What about this possibility ..."

Remember, positions are negotiable and the group needs to share its own pro and con responses so that it can decide on the merits of the *issue(s)* ... and avoid a focus on personalities.

If consensus cannot be reached, then resort to the democratic process and take a vote. Because you have endeavored to use the consensus process, you will find the majority opinion quite high. To resort to a democratic vote does not imply failure; rather, it announces the limits of consensus building and calls for a final accounting of the group opinion. *(Use Robert's Rules of Order Newly Revised, or search out the feminist version - Roberta's Rules of Order.)*

CONFLICT RESOLUTION

Conflict can be a creative dynamic. When conflict occurs, it invites the group to become more aware of the way the consensus process works. Conflict can offer an opportunity for growth and actually precipitate intimacy among the members if handled properly.

Many conflicts arise from miscommunication. One way to avoid conflict is for group members to actively listen to one another. Then, if miscommunication does occur, group members can clarify what was actually meant by each member involved in the conflict.

A few tips:

1. Separate people from the problem so individuals do not feel personally attacked.
2. Focus on the underlying interests and human needs of the persons in conflict, not on their stated positions.
3. Generate a variety of positions through brainstorming before deciding what to do.

To avoid conflict, use consensus techniques, such as:

Encourage participation – "How do you feel about this?" Ask for opinions - "What is your thinking on..."

Paraphrase – "Let me see if I understand your position ..."

Ask for a summary – "Will someone please summarize what we have agreed upon, and/or summarize the major objections?"

Ask for clarification – "It is not clear to me, please clarify ..."

Ask for examples – "Can you expand on that, perhaps giving some examples of what you mean?"

Test for consensus – "Before we go to the next issue, let's check to see if we all have agreed to…"

Initiate action – "How would you propose we proceed; any ideas on how we can get started?"

Action choices – "We must choose from three possible projects." "We have discussed both sides carefully, now we must choose."

Do a quick survey – "How many are in favor of this proposal?" "Let's see a show of hands."

Suggest a break – "We have been working on this problem for about an hour. I propose that we take a 10-minute break."

Suggest a procedure – "Let's go around the table and see how others feel…" or "Would it help if we put agenda items in rank order of importance before we go on?"

Share your feelings – "I'm feeling frustrated; I feel we should take this subject up next week. How do the rest of you feel?"

Be supportive – "Let's give XX a chance to speak…" or "YY, you had your say. Now it's ZZ's turn to speak."

Check goals – "Are we asking the right questions?" "Is this the only way to accomplish our task?"

Look into the future – "If we do it this way, what is the worst thing that could happen?" "If this works, how will it affect us later?"

Challenge differences – "I hear that XX doesn't agree, is that right?" "YY, you seem to be holding back. Is there something you disagree with?"

BAD VIBES? Confront by paraphrasing the unresolved conflicts. Ask participants to listen. Perhaps the issue(s) can be resolved by tabling until a later time or by forming a sub-group.

ACCOMPLISHMENTS
(Completing Tasks)

Every group needs to complete tasks if its members are to feel the group is worthwhile. In order to achieve concrete goals, members should take responsibility for making sure the following activities get done by the group as a whole.

(Warning: Be sure your goals are realistic!)

- **Exchanging Information:** offer facts, opinions, ideas and suggestions, and solicit the same from a variety of members.

- **Initiating Action:** propose goals and tasks that can lead to meeting these goals.

- **Setting Direction:** focus attention on the tasks and develop plans concerning how to proceed.

- **Summarizing:** pull together relevant ideas, suggestions, plans, and proposals; state major points.

- **Coordinating:** keep relationships clear between sub-groups, the larger group, and individuals, reminding group members of the relationship between the activities it is committed to, and propose next steps.

- **Reality-Testing:** examine the practicality and workability of plans, drawing on past experiences and history.

- **Evaluating:** compare group decisions and accomplishments with long-range goals, and analyze the implications for any future actions.

NURTURING RELATIONSHIPS
(The Soul of the Group)

Your group has an emotional life just as any individual does. Members of your group should be aware of what it takes to keep this emotional life healthy. The following list includes some major areas of concern.

• **Encourage Participation:** Support participation by recognizing contributions, and respecting the ways individual members feel comfortable participating.

• **Compromise and Harmonize:** Help turn conflicts into opportunities for creative solutions; remind group members to keep unity in mind during conflict.

• **Relieve Tension:** Create a safe and relaxed atmosphere by taking breaks, doing non-work-related activities, and laughing together.

• **Aid Communication:** To help eliminate misunderstandings, make sure that communication is accurate. Use "active listening" by repeating what you think the participant said.

• **Evaluate Emotional Climate**: Pay attention to how people are feeling about the group and each other.

• **Set Standards:** Re-state the group's goals so everyone understands the direction of the group's work, goals and accomplishments.

• **Promote an Open Atmosphere:** Support a relaxed openness so that members are not afraid to take risks when expressing themselves.

HOW TO BE A GOOD FACILITATOR

1. Never direct a group without its consent.

2. Make sure that 'roles' are fulfilled (e.g., Scribe, Light & Lively, Late-comer Briefer...).

3. Prepare for the meeting: Draw up an Agenda, remove distractions, check lighting and room temperature, etc. Have materials ready.

4. Keep discussions relevant. Be sure everyone knows the focus of the gathering, that it is their business being discussed and that everyone can contribute.

5. Keep track of time. If time is of the essence, request a time-keeper.

6. Be sure that topics, issues and goals are those that pertain to the whole group; encourage individuals to pursue their own topic on their own, or within a sub-group.

7. Show appreciation for progress and for special accomplishments.

8. Without eliminating humor, maintain an atmosphere in which people take each other seriously.

9. If people are bored... encourage them to speak, call for a Light-and-Lively, or suggest a break.

10. If someone is dominating ... ask others to state their opinions.

11. If someone keeps bringing up one idea ... let the person know she has been heard by paraphrasing the idea.

BENEFITS OF CO-FACILITATION

• More information and ideas are available during the planning.

• More energy (physical and emotional) is available to the group – especially during times of conflict or when handling complicated matters.

• If a facilitator becomes personally involved in the discussion, it is easy to hand the job over to the co-facilitator for the time being.

• Co-facilitation is a way for more people to gain experience and become skilled facilitators.

• It is less exhausting, demanding and scary.

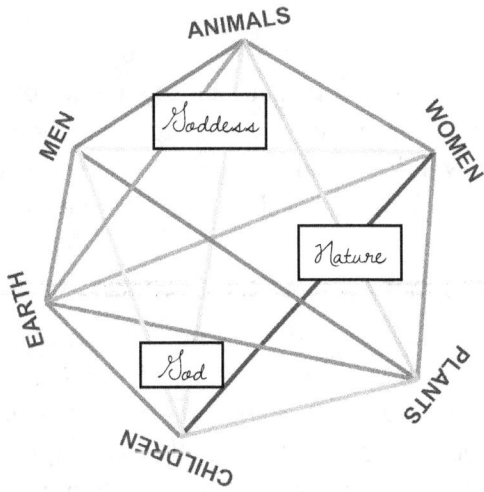

PLANNING EDUCATIONAL AND ACTION EVENTS

The following ideas and other "hot" topics can be addressed by using Shared Leadership to nurture the soul of the group and achieve goals.

Possible Topics

෴ Women's Reproductive Choice – This group has come together to plan an event that will support the local Planned Parenthood outreach campaign.

෴ Responding to Racism – The Social Justice committee as part of their anti-racism campaign wants the congregation to place a banner on the outside of the church. They also want to use it as a teaching tool.

෴ Planning an Earth-based Ritual – A group of members wants to provide to the entire congregation a solstice celebration at the church. Considerations include: Planning the components of the ritual; and who will do various aspects including setting up the room, greeting, providing refreshments, and so on.

The key to a successful planning meeting is to set an agenda with specific amounts of time for each item.
*The **Time Keeper** will help the group stay close to the allotted times on the agenda while the **Who-Speaks-Next Watcher** makes sure everyone has a chance to speak.*

Call for a "light and lively" if energy lags.

Before the meeting, select the **Co-Facilitators** to generate an Agenda. They should:

- Decide what information the group will need before they can begin, such as:

Suggestions for supporting Planned Parenthood:

✔ What are the laws now surrounding birth control and abortion?
✔ What statements/resolutions have the UUA and UUWF/UUWR made on the Right to Choose (see UUA website - summarize)?
✔ What services are provided by Planned Parenthood in your area – where are they located and whom do they mostly serve?
✔ *Note: You may want to invite a local/state representative of Planned Parenthood to give your group an update on their current status.*

Questions to stimulate discussion:

What ways can we support PP efforts in the community? How should we involve the congregation?

- Prepare an agenda. ***See sample on next page.*** *The underlined words/phrases and suggested times should be written on a large piece of paper and posted or duplicated and handed out to each participant.*

- Recruit a **Recorder** before the meeting if possible to keep a list of outcomes at the meeting.

Here's a sample agenda you can post for a meeting lasting less than 2 hours:

1. Opening (5 min) inspirational reading/poem/candle lighting.
2. Check-in (5 min) each person gives their name and a phrase highlighting why she/he came; then ask for volunteers for roles. (see pages 16-17)
3. Facilitators brief the group on context of the issue. (5 min)
4. Brainstorm possible activities (15 min) Use questions as prompts. **Scribe/Visual Aids Writer** writes ideas on sheets posted on the walls.
5. Break into Small Groups (10 min) of 2-3 members to prioritize the list.
6. Small groups report back (10 min) Reassemble into the whole group; **Scribe/Visual Aids Writer** places check marks next to popular items.
7. Break (10 min) – visit restroom, get beverage, stretch.
8. Entire group discussion (20 min) about ideas members like best and why.
9. Decision (15 min) Using consensus if possible, entire group makes decision and selects tasks needed. Otherwise vote. **Recorder** reads aloud the "education and action plan."
10. Feelings Check (10 min) to make sure everyone is "on board" with the outcome.
11. Volunteer for tasks. (5 min)
12. Process feedback from the **Process Observer.** (5 min)
13. Closing (5 min) – a song, chant, group hug. Extinguish candle.

A FEW BOOKS TO CONSIDER

The Millionth Circle: How to Change Ourselves and The World--The Essential Guide to Women's Circles by Jean Shinoda Bolen (excellent section on consensus)

Dealing with People You Can't Stand by Dr. Rick Brinkman and Dr. Rick Kirschner (classic guide, expanded edition)

The Chalice and the Blade: Our History, Our Future by Riane Eisler, now with an updated epilogue celebrating the 30th anniversary of this groundbreaking and increasingly relevant book.
(Also, any of her other publications)

Effective Meeting Skills by Marion E. Haynes (A fifty-minute series book)

The Female Advantage: Women's Ways of Leadership and *The Web of Inclusion* by Sally Helgesen

Leadership Skills for Women by Marilyn Manning (A fifty-minute series book)

Letting Go: Transforming Congregations for Ministry by Roy D. Phillips

Truth or Dare: Encounters with Power, Authority, and Mystery by Starhawk

UUA SEARCHABLE
LEADER LAB ARCHIVE
www.uua.org/leadership/blog/archive

Three examples from the Archive:

1) Collaborating Leadership
www.uua.org/leadership/blog/collaborating-leadership
Leaders in the future are going to be collaborators. They will understand that working with others builds a sense of ownership in problem-solving and future direction, and they will actively seek out others for conversation and discernment about issues that matter.

2) Emotionally Intelligent Leadership
www.uua.org/leadership/blog/emotionally-intelligent-leadership

During much of the last century, leadership was focused on intellect, reason, analysis, persuasion and the concept of experts. Leaders were admired and considered successful based on how forceful or decisive they were. Towards the end of the 20th century, however, we began to see the paradigm shifting. As more women were becoming leaders, leadership styles changed. There was a growing emphasis on collaboration and listening.

3) Culturally Competent Leadership
www.uua.org/leadership/blog/culturally-competent-leadership
Here in the United States, we have unfettered access to other people, cultures, thoughts, ideas. Even if we live in isolated communities, through the value of Internet and libraries and movies and television and radio, we "visit" with other people and get glimpses into the way others view the world. But chances are that unless we've done deep work to understand ourselves and our own cultures, including the assumptions we bring into every interaction, we will continue to view the world from our own perspective alone, complete with value judgments about how "they" are doing it "wrong."

ABOUT THE AUTHOR

Elizabeth Fisher has been a leader in the UU Women & Religion movement since the early 1980s. She is the author of the participatory course *Rise Up and Call Her Name: A Woman-honoring Journey into Global Earth-based Spiritualities* originally published by the Unitarian Universalist Women's Federation. In partnership with her husband Bob Fisher she presented workshops to fellowships, seminaries and churches over several decades, which helped to perfect this Circle Model. While developing the approach for *Rise Up*, Elizabeth collaborated with numerous contributors using Shared Leadership techniques. She also co-authored *Gender Justice: Women's Rights are Human Rights*, published by the Unitarian Universalist Service Committee, again sharing leadership.

Elizabeth holds a B.A. in Psychology, with dual minors in History and English from the University of Michigan (1969) and a Certificate in Publishing from the University of California (1986). She has worked in the fields of social work, law and publishing. As a writer and activist, she embraces diversity in human belief about divinity, and has spent considerable time exploring spiritual practices such as art, dance, visualization, song, storytelling, poetry, improvisation, study and reflection that honor the female divine around the world, from Anatolia, Africa, Asia, Europe and the Americas.

Her work can be found at: www.riseupandcallhername.com and www.lucilesrednotebook.org

ABOUT UU WOMEN and RELIGION

The Women and Religion Movement is alive and well in the 21st Century. A grassroots project started by lay leaders in the 1970s as an effort to promote examination of religious roots of sexism and patriarchy within the UUA and beyond, UU Women and Religion officially began as a task force following the unanimously-passed WOMEN AND RELIGION RESOLUTION at the 1977 UUA General Assembly. Although the Task Force was eventually sunsetted, the movement still exists in UU Districts that hold Women & Religion programs and woman-focused gatherings. It exists at General Assembly, where UUWR has an annual gathering and a booth in the display area. And it lives in the hearts and lives of women and men who have been touched by the many changes inspired by this movement. Find out more at www.UUWR.org

ABOUT THE CO-CONVENERS OF UUWR
Gretchen Ohmann and *Rev. "Twinkle" Marie Manning* are highly experienced and skilled in both the facilitation and practice of the Circle Model of Shared Leadership. They are available to present Shared Leadership workshops in a variety of locations, independently and as part of existing retreats and gatherings. **Please contact them at info@uuwr.org if you are interested in having a UUWR Shared Leadership worskshop or retreat.**

Gretchen Ohmann has been a UU since 1984, participating in her local Fellowship in SW Michigan over the years in worship arts, RE, board, newsletter, and as a music director, administrator, and bookkeeper. She's been involved in the UU Women and Religion movement since the mid-90s. Co-Convener and Storekeeper for UUWR, she runs the online store and travels all over the U.S. to bring those resources to UU women's events. Currently the part-time Technology Coordinator for the UUA MidAmerica Region, she also designs web sites for businesses and other UU groups and congregations. She's co-created and led worship services, musical performances, and workshops at UU gatherings such as District and Regional Assembly, SW UU Women's annual Conference, and in congregations other than her own.

www.ladyweave.com

Rev. "Twinkle" Marie Manning has been leading workshops and seminars in the secular and spiritual worlds for more than two decades. A seasoned event planner and television producer, she has honed the skills of project-creation and is comfortable interacting with audiences of all sizes. She is also a skilled ritualist and liturgist. She was the midwife to the Women's Goddess Covenant Circle at First Parish in Concord, MA, facilitator of Sacred Soul Sisters in California and is the visionary of Minerva Circles Online Gatherings. Twinkle is the Church of the Larger Fellowship's *Affiliate Community Minister for Women's Spirituality*.

As the Co-convener of UU Women and Religion, she is active in developing and leading programs that nourish women's spirituality. Twinkle is an interfaith minister serving regularly as pulpit resource for UU Congregations throughout New England. Her writings and poetry have been included internationally in all manner of worship services and publications. *Twinkle's Place* is approved as a UUA-related organization for Congregational Life.

www.TwinklesPlace.org

ADDITIONAL RESOURCES

The following pages contain Curriculum, Books and Programs
created and/or endorsed by UU Women and Religion.

www.uuwr.org

Rise Up & Call Her Name: A Woman-honoring Journey into Global Earth-based Spiritualities by Elizabeth Fisher is a 13 session journey where you will meet spiritual women, both earthly and divine, from around the world. Through creative rituals, music, readings, chanting, video, art, history, journaling and self-expression, you will be inspired to explore the female in her many colors within yourself and others. Powerful. Beautiful. Joyful.

The *Rise Up* journey can be done alone, with a significant other, or a cluster. It has been used by thousands of groups and individuals over twenty-five years. This material is intimate, heartfelt, and deeply personal, but it can also be a richly rewarding shared experience. Each session is 2-3 hours, modular segments so it is easily tailored to your time demands and interests.

The Kit contains: a detailed Leader's Guide with facilitation directions; a two-hour narrated video with multicultural images; a CD of songs, chants and instrumentals; and a lengthy Sourcebook of related information and inspiration.

More at **www.RiseUpAndCallHerName.com**
Order at: **www.uuwr.org/new-store/curricula**

The classic *Cakes for the Queen of Heaven* adult religious education curriculum offers a powerful gateway to awakening. Volume I is a reclaiming of the The Sacred Female, The Goddess Traditions and Women's Heritage of Peace containing five-sessions and features author Shirley Ranck's "Statement of Feminist Thealogy," Elinor Artman's "Brief Herstory of Cakes," and Nancy Vedder-Shults' "Baking Cakes for the Queen of Heaven."

The course continues in Volume II with six-sessions of exploration into the stories of powerful women found in ancient Judaism and in early Christianity.

Carole Etzler Eagleheart's CD *"She Calls to Us,"* contains many of the songs in the Cakes curriculum.

www.uuwr.org/new-store/curricula/cakes-curricula-1

A course for Unitarian Universalist adults and youths and our friends, published by UUWR in 2004. Course materials include a 100-page detailed course guide for co-leaders with handouts for participants. Topics in the seven two-hour sessions include gender, religion, feminism, economics, invisibility and denial, and how to challenge the patriarchal system.

Participants and co-leaders:
- Examine religious writings that influence our beliefs about women and men
- Study how the patriarchal system shapes women and men
- Identify and practice confronting patriarchal actions by organizations, other people, and ourselves

Participants learn that:
- We are not responsible for our inherited patriarchal system, and we participate in it.
- Paths of least resistance are easy to take and hard to recognize.
- We can change our attitudes and behavior, and can influence others.

www.uuwr.org/new-store/curricula/genderknot

These selections available at the UU Women and Religion online book store offer **rituals for all phases of a woman's life:** from *Meetings at the Moon* that provides opportunity for mothers and daughters to connect by sacred storytelling, creating sacred artifacts, singing and dancing together and *Goddess Gatherings* that offers thirteen sessions for a year of study in a circle of friends, to *Becoming Women of Wisdom: Marking the Passage into the Crone Years.* And, of course, in its original form: *The Water Ritual* that has become central to our UU faith tradition.

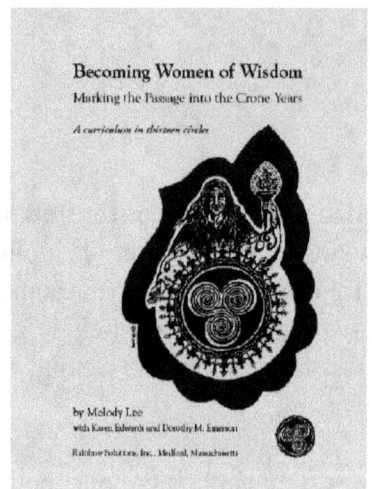

www.uuwr.org/new-store/curricula

Beautiful Song books and CDs by **Women With Wings UU Singing Group** brings the spiritual empowerment of women through voice. Their songs enhance consciousness of Mother Earth, express love for the environment and celebrate traditions from many cultures.

www.WomenWithWings.org

Molly Remer's **Womanrunes** book and card deck is inspired by women's spirituality foremother and wayshower, Shekhinah Mountainwater's creation of 41 woman-identified rune symbols for divination and personal growth. Womanrunes are a unique and powerful divination system that use simple, woman-identified symbols to connect deeply with your own inner wisdom as well as the flow of womanspirit knowledge that surrounds you.

www.BrigidsGrove.com/womanrunes

UU Talks is a new TED Talk-like initiative speakers-series that lifts up Unitarian Universalist voices and values.
UU Talks is designed as a unique way for congregations and groups to enhance their outreach and fundraising.

FIND OUT HOW
YOUR CONGREGATION OR GROUP *CAN HOST A UU TALK*
Join Us!
www.UUTalks.org
uutalkshome@gmail.com

Above pictured: Inaugural UU Talks event at the UUA in Boston
Peter Bowden, Matt Meyer, Lydia Edwards, Rev. Allison Palm,
Jim Tull, Anna Huckabee Tull, Regie Gibson, Marlon Carey,
Rev. Hank Pierce, Rev. "Twinkle" Marie Manning

MATRIKA PRESS SELECTIONS

ACCEPTING SUBMISSIONS

The Sophia Anthology Series

In the Spirit of Sophia Magazine, The Journal of Women and Religion, which was published by the Central Midwest District Women and Religion chapter from 1994 through 2004, UUWR is partnering with Matrika Press to create The Sophia Anthology Series where UU Women's stories and wisdom may be shared.

Submissions may include:
- essays, poetry, meditations, rituals
- customs, songs, chants, art
- personal stories
- experiences on your journey
- lessons you wish to share
- advice you wish to give
- myths (retold or created by you)
- the beauty of nature
- relationship to the divine
- how you honor your truth

www.MatrikaPress.com/SophiaAnthologySeries

UU Poets Series

Seasoned and emerging poets of all genres are invited to participate in this series.

www.MatrikaPress.com/UU-Poets-Society

ABOUT THE PUBLISHER

Matrika Press is an independent publishing house dedicated to publishing works in alignment with Unitarian Universalist Values and Principles. Its fiscal sponsor is UU Women and Religion, a 501c3 organization.

Matrika Press publishes anthologies, memoirs, poetry, prayer and ritual manuscripts, and other books to bring meaning and transformation to the world. A primary goal of Matrika Press is to publish stories and works that would otherwise remain untold. We also resurrect out-of-print manuscripts to ensure our historical works remain accessible.

Matrika Press titles are automatically made available to tens of thousands of retailers, libraries, schools, and other distribution and fulfillment partners, including Amazon, Barnes & Noble, Chapters/Indigo (Canada), and other well-known book retailers and wholesalers across North America, and in the United Kingdom, Europe, Australia and New Zealand and other Global partners.

For more information, visit:

www.MatrikaPress.com

ISBN:978-1-946088-09-3

www.ingramcontent.com/pod-product-compliance
Lightning Source LLC
Chambersburg PA
CBHW050205130526
44591CB00034B/2148